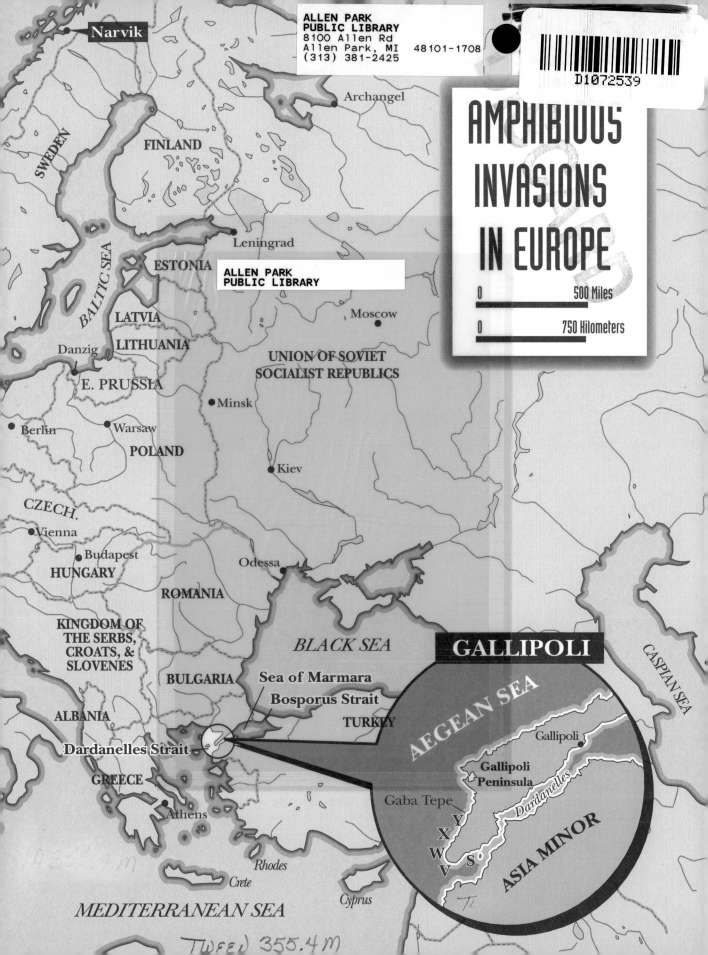

Tom McGowen

ASSAULT FROM THE SEA

AMPHIBIOUS INVASIONS IN THE TWENTIETH CENTURY

TWENTY-FIRST CENTURY BOOKS

Brookfield, Connecticut

To Marilyn Daleo
In gratitude for letting me talk to all those children

Cover photograph courtesy of Archive Photos
Photographs courtesy of Archive Photos: pp. 4, 14, 21, 60 (Popperfoto); Brown Brothers: pp. 7, 9, 39, 48, 51, 54; Hulton Getty/Archive Photos: pp: 11, 25, 28, 42, 52; New York Public Library Picture Collection: pp. 16, 19; U. S. Naval Institute: pp. 22, 30, 33, 38, 40; National Archives: p. 36 (#111-SC-1176486); Underwood Photo Archives, S.F.: pp. 56, 62

Library of Congress Cataloging-in-Publication Data
McGowen, Tom.
Assault from the sea : amphibious invasions in the twentieth century / Tom McGowen.
p. cm. — (Military might)
Includes index.
Summary: Outlines the history and development of troop carrier ships and amphibious vehicles, and describes how landing forces were used in some of the major battles of the twentieth century.
ISBN 0-7613-1811-9 (Lib. bdg.)
1. Amphibious warfare—History—20th century—Juvenile literature. [1. Amphibious warfare—History—20th century.] I. Title. II. Series
U261 .M38 2002 355.4'6'0904—dc21 2001041746

Published by Twenty-First Century Books
A Division of The Millbrook Press, Inc.
2 Old New Milford Road
Brookfield, Connecticut 06804
www.millbrookpress.com

Contents

1   A DISASTER CALLED GALLIPOLI   5

2   NORWAY AND ISLANDS IN THE PACIFIC   17

3   NORTH AFRICA AND SICILY   29

4   THE INVASIONS OF EUROPE   43

5   THE LANDING AT INCHON   57

     INDEX   64

Chapter 1

A DISASTER CALLED GALLIPOLI

Throughout history, in all parts of the world, the rumbling tread of marching armies invading a country was often heard. But there were times when the invading army did not march into another country, it *sailed* there. At these times, invasions came from the sea.

The first such invasion we know of was more than 3,000 years ago. Ships of invaders known only as "the Sea People," tried to sail up the Nile River into Egypt. Egyptian bowmen shot arrows into them from the shore, and Egyptian soldiers in boats attacked them in the river. The invasion was defeated. About 2,500 years ago, a Greek army defeated an invading Persian force on the shore of a place called Marathon, in Greece. Some 700 years ago, an invasion of Japan by China was defeated by the weather, when a violent windstorm destroyed many of the

British troops set up camp along the West Beach at Gallipoli.

Chinese ships. Invasions from the sea—amphibious invasions— were very risky. They could be destroyed by bad weather; they could be destroyed by an army waiting on the shore.

Before the twentieth century, there were a number of amphibious invasions. But in the twentieth century, when the two most widespread wars in history occurred, a great many invasions from the sea were attempted. Armies faced the problem of landing troops in places where the enemy was waiting for them with machine guns, artillery, and fortifications.

The first great sea invasion of the century was made during the First World War, which began in 1914. On one side were the Allies: France, Russia, Serbia, Belgium, and the British Empire, which included Canada, Australia, New Zealand, India, and a number of other countries now independent. On the other side were the Central Powers: the German Empire and the Austro-Hungarian Empire. In October, the Turkish Empire entered the war on the side of the Central Powers.

Most of Turkey is part of the Middle East, on the continent of Asia. But a tiny portion is in Europe, separated from the Asian part by the small inland Sea of Marmara. At the southern end of the sea is a narrow strip of water—a strait—called the Dardanelles, that leads to the Mediterranean Sea and southern Europe. At the northern end is another strait, the Bosporus, leading into another inland sea, the Black Sea, beyond which lies the coast of Russia.

If a fleet of enemy warships ever could have gained control of the Sea of Marmara, Turkey could have been cut in two. The Turks took steps to prevent this. The shores on either side of the narrowest part of the Dardanelles—a stretch less than a mile across, known as the Narrows—were dotted with fortresses containing many big, long-range cannons. The water was filled with strings of mines—underwater explosive devices that could blow a hole in any ship that touched one. No ships could get through

A view of the Bosporus Strait

the Narrows unless the Turks allowed them to and guided them past the mines.

This was a serious problem for Russia. The route through the Bosporus, the Sea of Marmara, and the Dardanelles was the only way Russia could receive supplies from the Allies or send things to them. With Turkey as an enemy, Russia's contact with its Western allies was cut off. It asked for help from the British and French.

They came up with a scheme to send a fleet of battleships into the Dardanelles. Battleships were the largest, most powerful warships at that time, with huge guns that could fire explosive missiles as much as 9 miles (14 kilometers). Such guns could pound the Turkish forts into ruins. The battleships would be preceded by smaller ships called minesweepers, which could cut loose mines in their path. It was believed the battleships would destroy the forts and move through the gaps in the mines into the Sea of Marmara and on to the Bosporus, opening the supply line between Russia and its allies, and cutting Turkey in two. Allied leaders believed that this move might even cause Turkey to surrender.

On February 19, 1915, a fleet of sixteen battleships accompanied by minesweepers entered the Dardanelles. Day by day, the warships moved forward. On March 18 they pushed into the Narrows. The battleships' huge guns began to batter the Turkish forts.

But things abruptly went wrong for the Allies. Within only a few hours three battleships were suddenly sunk, and three others badly damaged by mines. Believing this was done by cannon fire, the British commander called off the attack and pulled back. He sent word to Allied military commanders that the fleet could no longer advance unless a force of soldiers could be sent to wipe out or drive off the guns on the shore.

The shore along the northern side of the Dardanelles is the coast of a narrow strip of land known as Gallipoli Peninsula.

Guns on the British battleship Cornwallis
pound at the rocky shores at Gallipoli.

Allied commanders decided that an army landed on Gallipoli could move alongside the Dardanelles, wiping out the Turkish guns as it went. They made the decision to invade Turkey from the sea at Gallipoli.

Armies were made up of forces called divisions. A division was formed of about 12,000 riflemen, 4,000 artillerymen handling 72 cannons, and a number of other men who took care of various needs. The troops making up the army of invasion were a British army division, a French division, two combined Australian and New Zealand divisions, and a British naval division. This was about 78,000 men.

The army was assembled in Egypt, which was under British control. But through spies, the Turks were well aware of the planned invasion. By the time the Allied army arrived at Gallipoli, six Turkish divisions, about 84,000 men, were in position on the beaches and in the hills that lined the shores. In most places they had dug trenches: deep ditches in which they could stand and fire at enemy soldiers while they themselves were protected by the earth. In front of the trenches they stretched tangled webs of barbed wire along the beaches and in the shallow water. Up in the hills above the beaches were groups of cannons, ready to rain explosive shells down onto troops trying to land from the sea.

An invasion facing such obstacles had never been made before, and the Allies didn't quite know how to go about it. They planned to bring the soldiers to Gallipoli in battleships and simply load them into lifeboats and row them to the shore. However, they did construct one special sort of "landing ship," designed to put many soldiers ashore at once. Broad ramps were put on each side of a ship called *River Clyde*, which had been a coal carrier, and 2,000 soldiers were put aboard it. The idea was for it simply to sail straight onto the shore, deliberately going aground. Then the ramps would be lowered, and the soldiers could run down onto the beach.

The River Clyde *lands on the rocks at V Beach.*

The invasion fleet reached Gallipoli early on the morning of April 25, 1915. Each division had been assigned a certain place to land. The ships headed to their goals, and in the early morning darkness, the invasion began.

To try to fool the Turks, the French division and the British naval division made landings far from where the main landings would be made. They had no opposition, but they were too far away to be of any help to the troops making the main landings.

One of the main targets of the invasion was the "toe" of Gallipoli peninsula. There, at five places, termed beaches S, V, W, X, and Y, soldiers of the British 29th Division were to land and quickly move up into the rugged hills.

The landing at S Beach was a complete success. It was such a remote place that the Turks hadn't posted any soldiers to defend it.

At Y Beach, too, everything went remarkably well. Two thousand men landed without opposition, and climbed the cliffs that overlooked the beach. They saw no enemy soldiers.

But at V, W, and X beaches, the center of the 29th Division's attack point, the landing was a hideous, bloody disaster.

At dawn, the British battleship *Albion* began pounding the beaches with shells. This bombardment went on for an hour, until it seemed that nothing could be left alive. In full daylight, the *River Clyde* and twenty small boats filled with soldiers headed for the shore. The *River Clyde* slid up onto the beach.

Suddenly, there was a chattering roar of thousands of rifles and many machine guns. The Turkish soldiers, who had been sheltered among rocks up on the hills beyond the exploding shells, had come back down into their trenches on the beach and opened fire. Bullets were pouring into the boats!

In many boats, in just seconds, every man was either dead or dying. As men tried to clamber out of the boats they were hit and fell into the water. Soldiers began running down the ramps of the *River Clyde,* and many of them, too, were hit and dropped into the water. For 50 yards (46 meters) out from shore, the seawater turned blood-red.

Some men managed to get onto the beach and tried to keep going. Reaching the barbed wire, they couldn't get any farther. Many of them were hit, and the wire quickly became spotted with bodies, caught on the sharp barbs and hanging, dead and dying.

A few men survived. They lay hugging the ground, firing shots whenever they could, digging trenches to gain some shelter from the rifle and machine-gun fire ripping through the air at them.

A place farther up the coast, known as Gaba Tepe, was the target for the Australian and New Zealand divisions, which had been combined to form the Australian and New Zealand Army Corps—the ANZAC. They were brought in three battleships, and rowed to the shore in battleship lifeboats. Nothing happened until they were some 50 yards (46 meters) from the beach. Then, rifle fire began to crackle from the shore. The ANZACs leaped from the boats, waded onto shore, and launched a bayonet attack against the Turkish troops waiting for them hidden among the boulders on the rocky hillside. The Turks fled.

For a time, it seemed as if the ANZACs had control of things. Then, more Turkish troops arrived, with machine guns and cannons. A desperate, confused battle began, seesawing back and forth. To hold the ground they had taken, the ANZACs dug trenches for themselves, as the soldiers on the other beaches were doing.

Thus, by the end of the first day the British were badly hindered at their two main invasion points. Within the next few days, two rows of trenches ran along the beaches, in which the men faced each other day after day, shooting at each other. The invasion was stalled. The mission of the Allied soldiers—to move up into the hills and to wipe out the groups of cannons

Soldiers with bayonettes charge across the beach.

preventing the battleships from going through the Narrows—had become impossible.

In August, three more British divisions were sent to Gallipoli, and an attempt was made to launch a gigantic attack to break through the Turkish line. It was a failure. Allied military leaders realized there was no point in going on. Beginning in early December, Allied soldiers on Gallipoli were taken off by boats and loaded onto battleships, which sailed away. By January 9, 1916, all were gone.

More than a quarter of a million Allied soldiers had died or been wounded on Gallipoli. The Turks lost nearly as many, but they had won: They had prevented the invasion of their country. The Allies had lost men, lost ships, and lost the chance to help Russia. For them, the first sea invasion of the twentieth century had been a disaster.

Chapter 2

NORWAY AND ISLANDS IN THE PACIFIC

The Second World War began in Europe in 1939, when German troops invaded Poland. Great Britain and France quickly declared war on Germany, and the most terrible war in history was under way.

Poland was quickly conquered. Then, for a time, nothing much took place. There was no fighting at all.

But in April of 1940, Germany suddenly launched another invasion—an amphibious one. The target was Norway. Having Norway under its control would give Germany a number of advantages in the war.

The invasion was based almost completely on surprise. On the morning of April 9, five small fleets, each of several German warships and ships carrying German troops, sailed for five

Wrecked German ships lie in Narvik Bay following an attack by British warships during the German invasion of Norway.

Norwegian ports. Each arrived at its target in early morning darkness.

At the port of Narvik, German warships torpedoed two Norwegian coast-guard vessels that tried to stop them, sailed past the sinking hulks, and landed 2,000 troops in the port. At the port of Trondheim, a Norwegian coast defense gun opened fire on the suspicious German ships heading into the port. A German heavy cruiser quickly knocked the gun out with its own big guns. German troops were successfully landed in Trondheim, too.

At Kristiansand, coast defense guns also opened fire on the mysterious ships that had suddenly appeared. The German fleet pulled back and called for help from the air force. Before long, bombers appeared, and the Norwegian shore guns were destroyed. German troops were soon landed.

At the port of Bergen, the Germans tricked the port's defenders into believing they were British ships on a friendly visit. By the time the trick was detected, German troops were in the city.

But at Oslo, Norway's capital and biggest port, the Germans ran into trouble. Here, too, coast defense guns opened up as the invasion fleet steamed toward the harbor, but these did some harm. A German battleship was badly damaged, and a cruiser was sunk.

However, the invading force simply turned around, moved about 12 miles (19 kilometers) down the coast, and landed the troops there. They moved forward, and pushed into Oslo. Shortly, German paratroopers were floating down into the city to help them, and Oslo was soon in German hands.

Thus, the first amphibious invasion of the war was a success. The little Norwegian army was no match for German forces, and was soon put out of action. The British and French tried to go to Norway's rescue, landing troops in several places, but they couldn't match the German buildup and eventually had to be pulled back out. The German conquest of Norway was complete.

Soldiers of the invading German army in Norway operate a machine gun.

In May, Germany invaded the Netherlands, Belgium, and France. By the end of June, all three nations were conquered. Germany and Italy had formed an alliance, known as the Axis, and Britain now stood alone against it.

Germany's military leaders began planning an invasion of Britain. Of course, it would have to be an amphibious invasion—German forces would have to cross the English Channel, the narrow strip of sea between Britain and France. Preparations began, but soon were called off. An invasion of Britain from the sea in 1940 never took place.

However, when the war spread to the Pacific Ocean in 1941, there was a flurry of successful sea invasions. There are thousands of islands scattered throughout the Pacific Ocean, from tiny piles of rock to large areas of land with mountains, rivers, and forests. The United States, Great Britain, and Japan all held many of these as naval and military bases, where troops were stationed, warships could go for fuel, supplies, and water, and airplanes were kept and maintained. When the United States was drawn into war on December 7, 1941, with a giant Japanese air attack on the American naval base at Pearl Harbor, Hawaii, Japanese army and navy forces made surprise amphibious invasions of many American and British bases. Caught by surprise and overwhelmingly outnumbered, the defenders of the bases invariably had to surrender.

As 1942 began, things looked very bad for the Americans and their allies, the British and the Dutch. But then, in June, the Japanese attempted an invasion of the important American base at Midway Island. American warships were there to prevent the invasion, and in one of the great sea battles of history, the Americans smashed the Japanese attack. This was a tremendous victory that turned things in America's favor and soon after, the United States began a campaign of its own to invade Japanese island bases.

The U.S. Navy and Marine Corps had studied the invasion of Gallipoli, and learned from its mistakes. They realized that a special kind of boat was needed for getting troops to shore *fast* and landing them quickly. Special crafts also were needed solely to bring in vehicles and supplies. By 1942 several kinds of vessels were available for amphibious landings. Some were small boats such as the Landing Craft, Personnel, or LCP, which could carry thirty-six men or four tons of supplies, and the Landing Craft, Vehicle, or LCV, which could bring thirty-six men or a small vehicle such as a light truck, onto shore. These crafts were carried on ships, and lowered into the water for

*During the battle at Midway Island, June 4, 1942,
U.S.S.* Hornet *aircraft strike at a Japanese cruiser.*

A Landing Craft, Vehicle (LCV); notice the small ramp that drops down for quick delivery of soldiers and a small vehicle to the shore.

action. They were built of light plywood, driven by diesel engines, and designed to run up into the shallow water at the edge of a beach. Marines would then leap out and splash up onto land. Because most of these crafts were built by a company called Higgins, they were generally known as Higgins boats.

The first target of an American amphibious invasion was a cluster of four small-to-tiny islands—Florida Island, Tulagi, Gavutu, and Tanambogo—and a fairly large one nearby, called Guadalcanal. These were in the group of islands known as the

Solomons, about 1,000 miles (1,609 kilometers) northeast of Australia. The Japanese had a few troops on some of these islands. They were also building an airfield on Guadalcanal, from which they would be able to send planes to attack ships going to and from Australia. American military leaders agreed this had to be prevented. Guadalcanal had to be taken over so the Japanese couldn't use the airfield, and the other islands had to be cleared of Japanese troops.

The troops selected for this work were the First Division of the United States Marine Corps, the First Marine Raider Battalion, and the First Marine Parachute Battalion. This totaled about 19,000 men (there were no women in any American combat units at that time). The invasion force was assembled as secretly as possible in the Fiji Islands, northeast of Australia. It consisted of nineteen U.S. Navy troop-transport ships and supply ships protected by forty-three warships— destroyers, cruisers, and three U.S. aircraft carriers. On July 31, 1942, this force set out for the Solomon Islands.

It arrived in darkness at two o'clock on the morning of August 7. It split into two parts; one moving toward Guadalcanal Island, the other heading to the cluster of four small islands. By six o'clock both groups were in position. Unlike Gallipoli, where the Turks were ready and waiting for the invasion, the Japanese troops on the islands were completely unaware they were about to be attacked.

They quickly became aware. At 6:14, a sudden thunder of guns shattered the silence as American warships began raining shells onto the buildings and installations the Japanese had put up on Guadalcanal and Tulagi. The roar of eighty-five airplane engines added to the din, as planes from the aircraft carriers raced over the islands, bombing and machine-gunning any-thing that seemed a good target. Japanese seaplanes and boats in Tulagi's harbor were destroyed, docks were shattered, and barracks on Guadalcanal were demolished. The Japanese sol-diers fled into the jungles and rocky hills.

The decks of the transport ships were crowded with waiting marines. Huge nets of thick rope were stretched across the sides of the transports. These served as rope ladders down which scores of marines quickly scrambled into the Higgins boats waiting in the water below, beside the ships' hulls.

Florida Island was first to be invaded. There were no Japanese there, and no resistance for the 183 marines who landed at 7:40.

Tulagi was next. There were 1,500 Japanese troops there, and two destroyers and a cruiser moved near shore and began dropping shells everywhere along the beach Japanese soldiers might be hiding. Higgins boats moved quickly toward shore, but encountered an unsuspected coral reef some distance from the beach and were unable to go all the way. The men of the First Marine Raider Battalion had to wade ashore from water up to their armpits. The first men were on the beach at almost exactly eight o'clock, and by 8:30 were advancing into the jungle in a long line. Not a shot had been fired yet. As the leading Raider companies moved forward, troops of the Second Battalion of the 5th Marine Regiment reached the beach and followed them.

It was around this time, about 9:09, that the main invasion of Guadalcanal Island took place. Eleven thousand marines were carried to the beach in Higgins boats. Shells from the guns of destroyers and cruisers moaned through the air over them, exploding on the beaches and in the jungle beyond. In the foaming surf at the edge of the beach, the marines leaped from the boats and surged onto the shore. They rushed across the sand toward the jungle and moved cautiously into the tall palm trees. Behind them, more boats and landing ships were bringing more men, artillery, trucks, tanks, and supplies.

On Tulagi, the lines of marines moved steadily forward. Two hours passed. Then the marines reached the point where the Japanese troops were dug in. From holes in the ground,

*Pouring out from a fleet of Higgins boats, marines land
on the beaches of Guadalcanal, September 7, 1942.*

from treetops, from the mouths of caves, the Japanese opened up with rifle fire, machine guns, and mortars (small cannons). The marines moved forward methodically, wiping out the Japanese among the trees with rifle fire, and throwing grenades and satchel charges—clusters of high explosives in bags—into caves where they were holed up. By nightfall, most Japanese on Tulagi had been wiped out, and the marines had taken the island.

While the marines on Tulagi were battling, the invasion of Gavutu Island began. At 11:45 A.M., destroyers and a cruiser shelled Gavutu's beach, and shortly after, the first boats carrying the 351-man Marine Parachute Battalion reached the shore. The men sprang out and charged across the beach. Only one was hit, by a bullet that instantly killed him.

But as the next four Higgins boats reached shore they ran into a hail of rifle and machine-gun fire. There were Japanese troops on a hill overlooking the beach, and they now opened up with everything they had.

The marines rushed forward and took up positions around the hill. Gradually, they worked their way upward, wiping out the Japanese troops in their path. By late afternoon, the Americans were in control of the tiny island.

About 500 yards (457 meters) from Gavutu lies the equally tiny island of Tanambogo. In 1942 the two were connected by a causeway—a long, narrow road made of crushed coral raised above the seawater. At 6:00 at night, marines tried to go over the causeway and capture Tanambogo. They ran into such heavy rifle and machine-gun fire that they had to pull back and ask for help from American and Australian warships out in the water beyond the islands. The ships pounded Tanambogo with gunfire, but it finally took an attack across the causeway by a whole marine battalion with tanks to wipe out all Japanese resistance.

Thus, by nightfall, Florida Island had been taken, Gavutu had been taken, Tanambogo had been taken, and troops and supplies were building up on Guadalcanal. But on Tulagi, heavy fighting was still taking place. At twilight, the marines dug in, making small shallow ditches called foxholes in which a man could crouch, somewhat protected from rifle fire. During the night, the Japanese launched fierce attacks, the officers slashing with swords and the men stabbing with bayonets. The marines beat them off with rifle fire and grenades.

In the morning, the marines moved forward into a region where Japanese soldiers, holed up in caves and crevices, kept up a steady fire. They were determined to die fighting. When they refused to surrender, the marines wiped them out with grenades and satchel charges. By the end of the day, Tulagi was cleared of Japanese troops.

It seemed that the invasion was successful. But the fighting was not over. The Japanese high command resolved to recapture Guadalcanal, and sent troops to reinforce those on the island. For seven months, battles raged on Guadalcanal and in the sea around it. Finally, the Japanese commanders decided it was impossible to retake Guadalcanal. Japanese ships began sneaking to points along the coast each night, and by February 9, 1943, had managed to remove all their troops from the island.

The successful invasion and capture of Guadalcanal and the other four islands actually ended all further Japanese attempts to seize more islands. But for America, it was only the beginning of a long advance toward Japan. Using what had been learned from the invasion of Guadalcanal, American forces began to make one amphibious invasion after another of Japanese island bases—Tarawa, Kwajalein, Eniwetak, Guam, Saipan, Tinian, Peleliu, the Philippine islands of Leyte and Luzon, and finally the islands of Iwo Jima and Okinawa, close to Japan itself. Most of these invasions were bitterly opposed, often by troops in strongly fortified positions, with plenty of artillery and machine guns. Most were bloody and hard fought, especially Iwo Jima, where the U.S. Marines took some 25,000 casualties, and Okinawa, where nearly 50,000 Americans were killed and wounded. But all were American victories.

Chapter 3

NORTH AFRICA AND SICILY

While naval battles and amphibious invasions were taking place in the Pacific Ocean in 1942, tank battles were raging in North African deserts. A British army was locked in combat with an Axis (German and Italian) army. On November 8, 1942, an American and British force, under the command of U.S. General Dwight D. Eisenhower, made a giant surprise invasion of North Africa from the sea to bring help to the British. The invasion came to be known as Operation Torch.

The invasion force of more than 107,000 men was organized in three groups and came from two directions. The first group, the Eastern Task Force, consisted of about 23,000 British troops and 10,000 American troops. Guarded by British warships, it sailed from Britain to the coast of the North African country of Algeria. The second group, the Center Task Force, was formed entirely of about 39,000 American troops, two divi-

General Dwight D. Eisenhower (center), General Harold Alexander (left), and Lieutenant General George Patton confer during Operation Torch.

This LST (Landing Ship, Tank) receives a group of fighting men headed toward the shores of North Africa and eventually, Sicily.

sions, and also sailed from Britain. Its target was the port city of Oran, in Morocco, just west of Algeria.

The third group, the Western Task Force, comprised of about 35,000 men, was also made up of two American divisions, and was also headed for Morocco. But it sailed from Norfolk, Virginia, across the Atlantic Ocean—the first time in history a military invasion force ever crossed an entire ocean.

The fleets carried Higgins boats for troop landings, but this army also had tanks to land, and both the British and Americans had special ships to carry them. The British ships were two oil tankers that had been given broad flat fronts that could be dropped open to form a ramp down which a tank could drive onto shore. The Americans adapted the kind of ship used for delivering railroad cars from one country to another to carry tanks.

In 1942, Morocco and Algeria were French colonies. Although France had been conquered by Germany and half of it was occupied by German troops, it still controlled these colonies, and they were guarded by French army troops and French navy warships. Allied agents and diplomats had been at work to convince French leaders to allow Allied troops to land in the colonies and to join them in fighting the Germans and Italians. Most French hated the Germans, and the Americans expected French forces in Morocco and Algeria would welcome them with open arms.

Things did not work out that way. The ships of Eastern Task Force arrived off the coast of Algeria shortly after midnight on November 8. A British commando (special force) unit moved toward the shore in Higgins boats. Suddenly, searchlights began to blink on along the beach. Red flashes lit up the night, and cannon shells began to explode in the water around the boats. The French were firing on the Allies!

British warships fired back at the shore guns. Two British destroyers raced toward the port to try to land an American infantry regiment in the city. One was hit so badly it began to take in water and had to turn back out to sea. The other managed to land 250 soldiers, but it, too, was badly damaged and had to withdraw. With no more troops coming to help them, the 250 American soldiers who had been landed were forced to surrender. Outside the city of Algiers, the British and American troops who had come ashore were stalled before a fortress manned by French troops, unable to advance. Eastern Task Force's landing had turned into a calamity!

Center Task Force's landing was considerably easier. The American 1st Infantry Division went ashore on one side of Oran, the 1st Armored Division landed on the other side. They began to move toward the city with almost no opposition from French troops—yet.

But then, the French navy decided to make a stand. Two British ships trying to take American Rangers into Oran harbor were suddenly under fire from French warships in the harbor. One was sunk, the other actually blown out of the water.

A full-scale battle erupted. A British battleship and two cruisers opened fire on the French ships and the city. French planes appeared in the sky to attack advancing American troops and were quickly driven off by British planes. The British planes then bombed and machine-gunned French troops massing to stop the American advance, scattering them. The Americans pushed forward into Oran, and gradually, French troops began to surrender. Center Task Force had taken its objective.

The ships of Western Task Force reached their position a little before midnight. The landing forces were supposed to make for three points on shore: two north of the city of Casablanca, and one to its south. But when the Higgins boats began going to shore, they became hopelessly mixed up, and many went to the wrong place. Some capsized in the surf, spilling men and supplies into the water. French troops on the beaches might have inflicted terrible casualties. Luckily for the Americans, the French troops were farther back, lying in wait.

As the sun began to rise the next morning, French coastal defense cannons on the shore and a French battleship in Casablanca harbor opened up on the ships that could now dimly be seen. The American ships began to rip the air with salvos from their own big guns and soon silenced both shore guns and the battleship. A group of French destroyers came

A U.S. Coast Guard landing craft brings the Royal British Marines to the coast of North Africa.

charging out of the harbor to attack the American troop transports and landing craft. The American warships sank two of them; American aircraft carrier bombers sank two others. By noon, the naval battle was over, and all was silent.

On the shore, American troops had moved toward Casablanca, wiping out or taking prisoner French troops who attempted to stop them. The commander of the two divisions,

General George Patton, made his way into Casablanca, met with French leaders, and offered terms for surrender that they quickly accepted. The Western Task Force had accomplished its job, and the fighting in Morocco was over.

Meanwhile, in Algiers, American agents managed to contact a French admiral and persuaded him to order a cease-fire. In Algeria, too, the fighting was over.

In a short time, French troops actually became part of the force they had been fighting against. Their leaders declared that French forces in Africa would now join the Allied army to help fight for the freedom of their homeland. Unfortunately, many Frenchman and a thousand Allied soldiers had been killed in battles that need not have taken place.

The Axis troops in North Africa were now trapped between the British army in the east and the Allied forces that had landed in the west. They could not hold out against these forces pushing at them from two sides. On May 6, 1943, completely surrounded and with their backs to the sea, they began to surrender by the hundreds of thousands. North Africa and the whole Mediterranean Sea were now under Allied control.

Even before this victory, Allied leaders had met to discuss what their next step should be. There were two different ideas.

The Americans wanted a decisive battle to bring the war in Europe to a quick end. They urged building up a huge force of men, tanks, planes, and ships in Britain, and launching a major sea invasion against German forces in France to drive them back into Germany.

But the British didn't think Allied forces were strong enough for such an operation yet. Germany's partner, Italy, was much weaker than Germany, so the British suggested making a move against Italy. If Italy appeared to be in danger, Germany would have to pull many of its divisions out of France into Italy to help defend it. This would weaken German forces in France so that perhaps the Allies could eventually attack there.

In time, American leaders agreed. It was decided to make a threatening move against Italy by invading the island of Sicily.

Italy is shaped somewhat like a boot sticking down into the Mediterranean Sea, and the rocky, mountainous island of Sicily, about the size of Vermont, lies just off the boot's "toe," no more than 2 miles (3 kilometers) from the coast. It is part of the Italian nation, and an invasion of Sicily would certainly present a serious threat to Italy.

However, Sicily contained 3 naval bases, 19 military airfields, 200,000 Italian troops with a small force of tanks, and 30,000 Germans in 2 special divisions. One was an armored infantry division of about 40 tanks and 2 infantry regiments, and the other was a panzer (armored) division, with about 100 tanks and 3 infantry regiments. The infantrymen were specially trained troops who went into battle in armored vehicles. An invasion of Sicily would not be easy.

Furthermore, Allied leaders knew, from spies, that most German and Italian leaders expected Sicily to be invaded. German and Italian units had been put on alert, ready to be rushed to the island if necessary. Allied leaders decided that some trickery was needed, to make enemy leaders think Sicily was not an invasion target.

A British soldier who had died was dressed as an officer, and a briefcase was chained to his wrist, indicating that he was a special messenger. In the briefcase were fake documents revealing that the Allies intended to invade either Greece or the Italian island of Sardinia, both of which were occupied by German and Italian troops. The body was put into the sea off the coast of Spain. It was discovered and taken to Spanish officials, who believed this was a British officer who had drowned in an accident at sea. Many Spaniards wanted Germany and Italy to win the war, and someone opened the briefcase and gave copies of the documents to Axis spies. Thus, most German and Italian leaders soon began to disregard the possibility of an invasion of

Warships, troopships, and landing craft are assembled during preparations to cross the Mediterranean into Sicily.

Sicily, and urged preparation for an invasion of Greece or Sardinia. The trick had worked!

On the night of July 8, the Allied invasion force began to leave from ports on the North African coast. This was the biggest amphibious invasion yet. Two armies totaling some 160,000 men—the American Seventh Army, commanded by General Patton, and the British Eighth Army of General Sir Bernard Montgomery—were carried to Sicily from North African ports by more than 3,000 ships, including 500 warships.

The movement of so many ships could not be kept secret, and German air patrols reported them early on July 9. So the Axis military leaders knew the invasion was about to happen, but there was no way to tell for sure *where*. Greece? Sicily? Sardinia?

The landings were scheduled for early morning on July 10, but during the night some 3,400 American paratroopers of the 82d Airborne Division and about 1,200 glider troops of the British 1st Airborne Landing Brigade came down on Sicily ahead of the amphibious forces. They blew up bridges and railroad tracks, cut telephone wires, and seized crossroads, preparing the way for the two armies. German and Italian generals began getting reports of all this, and knew the invasion had begun in Sicily. They started sending troops to places they thought most likely to be hit.

As the amphibious forces arrived that morning, 1,700 landing craft began carrying troops to shore. The Allies had learned from the invasion of North Africa, and many landing craft were new kinds of vessels that had been built since then. One was the Landing Craft, Personnel (Ramp), or LCP(R), which could run up onto a beach, where its entire bow (front) would instantly drop open, forming a ramp down which men could rush out onto land. The fronts and sides of these boats were built of steel, providing protection from bullets. Another new craft was the DUKW, a boat with wheels, which could

*This amphibious "duck" (DUKW), essentially a watercraft
with wheels, was at home on land or at sea.*

plough through the water at about 6 miles (10 kilometers) an
hour, then drive right up onto land and speed on at 50 miles
(80 kilometers) an hour there. It could carry 25 men or 5,000
pounds (2,270 kilograms) of supplies. Still another important
new craft was the large, oceangoing Landing Ship, Tank, or
LST, which could bring in five 40-ton tanks or other vehicles
and large amounts of supplies.

The British army's landing place was on Sicily's southeastern coast, which caught the Italian and German commanders by surprise. They had not expected it there, and the landing was unopposed. Moving fast, the British captured the large, important port of Syracuse, and began using it to land more troops, tanks, and supplies quickly.

The landing point for the American army was a long stretch of beach along Sicily's southern coast, with the small port of Gela at its center. It turned out to be a hard landing to make.

This U.S. Coast Guard LST is loaded with trucks and supplies.

A fleet of LSTs on the docks of a North African port

The night was stormy in this area, and strong winds pushed many ships off course and made it difficult to lower landing crafts. Along the shore, big Italian coast-defense guns began to open up, firing on the dimly seen ships. American warships answered with their own big guns, and before long had knocked the Italian guns out. As the LCPs and other craft moved shoreward, the American warships kept up a steady blaze of fire, pounding the beaches where the troops would land.

It was 9 miles (14 kilometers) through choppy water to the beaches, and many soldiers became violently seasick. By the time the beaches were reached, many of the drenched, vomiting men were in no condition to do any fighting. They would have been doomed had any enemy troops been waiting for them. However, believing the sea was too rough for a landing to be made on this night, most of the Italian troops guarding the coast were sleeping in their quarters. Only at Gela did the American troops assigned to capture the town have to do any fighting. Otherwise, for half an hour, the Americans had an unopposed landing. More and more troops came ashore; LSTs brought in tanks; and DUKWs delivered supplies and ammunition.

Then Italian and German troops began arriving. A small force of Italian tanks came clattering into Gela. The Americans in the town knocked one out with an antitank gun, and drove the rest off. Next, 600 Italian infantrymen tried to make an attack, but were also driven off, with rifle and machine-gun fire.

The German panzer division was also speeding toward Gela. This was a serious danger, for the tanks and the infantrymen in their armored vehicles would be able to slaughter the Americans on the open beach and drive them back into the sea. The invasion could be defeated.

But as the tanks began to come within sight of the beach, the U.S. warships offshore opened up with their big guns. Shells rained down, knocking tanks over and blowing them apart. The division commander ordered a withdrawal, and the tanks and other vehicles turned and scuttled back the way they had come.

The danger to the landing forces was over, and the buildup of men, vehicles, and supplies continued. The Axis troops had lost their only chance of pushing Allied forces off the island, and the invasion of Sicily had been successfully accomplished.

Chapter 4

THE INVASIONS OF EUROPE

The battle to capture all of Sicily took thirty-eight more days, ending August 17, 1943, when the German and Italian commanders took their troops off the island and went to Italy. The Allied capture of Sicily caused a major change in the war. In 1943 Italy was a kingdom, but it was controlled by a dictator, Benito Mussolini, known as "The Leader." Mussolini's form of government, like Adolf Hitler's in Germany, was fascism, with everything people did carefully controlled, and little if any freedom. The Italian people had grown sick of fascism and weary of the war. So when the Allies showed their military might by capturing Sicily, Mussolini was deprived of power and placed under arrest. Soon after, representatives of the Italian king secretly met with Allied leaders and announced Italy's willing-

Italian dictator Benito Mussolini (left) and Adolf Hitler, the leader of Nazi Germany ness to sign an armistice—an agreement to stop fighting—and drop out of the war.

This was a tremendous victory for the Allies, knocking Germany's major partner out of the war and apparently opening up Italy for an unopposed invasion. An invading army could push north through Italy into German territory.

The Allied invasion plan was to land at three separate places a few days apart. On September 3, General Montgomery's British Eighth Army crossed over from Sicily to the "toe" of Italy, landing in the region called Calabria. There was no opposition.

On September 8, the newly formed U.S. Fifth Army, consisting of two American and two British divisions, and commanded by American General Mark Clark, sailed from North Africa. It would land on the "ankle" of the boot, about 130 miles (210 kilometers) north of the Eighth Army, at the large seaport of Salerno. At the same time, a British division would land on the "heel" of the boot, at the port of Taranto.

As the troop ships headed toward Italy, the armistice was announced throughout the country, and the Italian army was instructed not to fight. However, the Germans had been expecting the Italians to desert them. They had been quietly bringing more and more troops into Italy, and now they took control of the country. Italy, like France, became an occupied country, with a strong force of tough, experienced German troops taking the place of the country's army. The German soldiers felt that by fighting to prevent an invasion of Italy, they were helping to prevent an eventual invasion of their own country.

The German commander had believed the main Allied attack would be at Salerno, and had his forces ready there. As the Fifth Army assault boats began landing at Salerno, hidden machine guns began to crackle, and the beach was pounded by explosions of mortar shells and the terrible 88 mm-cannons of the German army. Luftwaffe fighter planes roared over the beach, machine-gunning the incoming troops. By nightfall, the Fifth Army was barely hanging on to only four separate areas of the beach.

For the next two days the fighting at the beach continued, with the Allied troops desperately holding on in some places and inching forward only a little in others. The German commanders were determined to smash the invasion and inflict a humiliating defeat on the Allies. On September 13, they launched a furious attack. Panzer divisions led by Germany's formidable Tiger tanks began to rumble forward, smashing through the Allied soldiers until they were only 2 miles (3 kilometers) from the edge of the sea. General Clark had to face the possibility that he would have to bring in ships and pull his army off the beach or have it wiped out.

The German tanks were finally stopped from pushing the almost helpless infantry back into the sea by the cannons of the U.S. 45th Division artillery and the Allied warships. The cannons were lined up only 10 yards (9 meters) apart and when the German tanks began appearing, the guns opened up at point-blank range. Firing every twenty seconds, the gunners slammed shells into the tanks. From out on the water, the guns of warships joined in. As darkness fell, the tanks and German troops began to pull back, unable to keep going through the rain of fire.

The crisis was over. More and more men and supplies began to pile up on the Salerno beaches. Waves of Allied bombers flew over the area, pounding every German position they saw. The British Eighth Army was slowly fighting its way up from the south. The Germans pulled out of the Salerno area and withdrew northward.

Of all the Allied amphibious invasions of World War II, the invasion of Italy came closest to turning into another Gallipoli. But once German forces began to withdraw, the success of the invasion was assured. However, there were still months and months of hard, bloody fighting as the Allies slowly pushed forward.

Meanwhile, in Britain, the Allies were building up a gigantic force for the biggest sea invasion of the war, the biggest sea invasion of world history, and the most immense and complicated military operation that ever took place. More than 4,000 troop ships and landing craft, accompanied by 600 warships, would carry 176,000 men to the French coast and put them ashore there.

The German leader, Adolf Hitler, and his generals knew the invasion was coming, and were sure it would be sometime between May and August. But they didn't know where it would hit, and so they had an enormous length of shoreline to defend—the coasts of Holland and Belgium, and the northern, western, and southern coasts of France. They did not have enough troops to defend along that entire area, so they had to decide the most likely places for the invasion and fortify those.

Some generals believed the invasion would come across the narrowest part of the Channel, which would make things easiest for the Allies. This would hit a part of the French coast called Pas de Calais. But Hitler believed it would come across the *widest* part of the channel, to the region called Normandy, to try for a surprise.

Hitler was right. The Allied commanders had chosen Normandy as the place of invasion. But, as they had done for the invasion of Sicily, the Allies used trickery to try to fool the Germans. In the part of England directly across from Pas de Calais, thousands of tanks, trucks, and cannons were gathered together. Any spy seeing this mass of vehicles and weapons would be convinced it was the buildup for an invasion at Pas de Calais. But the weapons and vehicles were all fakes, made of rubber and plywood! Meanwhile, the real weapons and equipment for the Normandy invasion were quietly being gathered at various places, and often disguised to look like other things.

It had been decided the invasion must be made on either June 5, 6, or 7, 1944. The tide would be lowest then, and a lot of the obstacles the Germans had put along the shore underwater, to prevent boats from landing, would be revealed and could be avoided. It was hoped that on these three days the sea would be calm and visibility good.

But as June began, the first few days were stormy, with wind that turned the sea choppy. This would make the landings difficult. Allied leaders were worried. If the invasion had to be postponed, it would be a whole month before conditions were right again. The Germans would surely find out about the invasion by then, and would be prepared for it.

Then, meteorologists determined that one day, June 6, *might* have sufficiently good enough weather to make the invasion possible. It was a risk that General Eisenhower decided he had to take.

The Allied plan was to land two armies at five main points along 50-mile (80-kilometer) stretch running from east to west on the Normandy coast. Farthest east, the British 2d Army would land at beaches designated Juno, Sword, and Gold. To the west, the 1st U.S. Army would land at Utah Beach and Omaha Beach.

By the night of June 5, the thousands of ships carrying the invasion force were moving through the heaving sea toward France. Again, seasickness was a problem. But this time the troops had been given brown paper bags to throw up in, instead of having to use their helmets!

The British troops were preceded by several different kinds of tanklike vehicles especially designed to counteract German defenses. Some of these were tanks with a huge club on their front, which beat the ground to make buried mines explode.

A fleet of U.S. ships heads toward the coast of Normandy for the D-Day invasion, June 6, 1944. Above the ships are huge balloons, attached by a cable, to protect against airplane attack.

Others were tanks equipped with flamethrowers that could hurl a fiery jet 120 yards (110 meters) to wipe out enemy pillboxes (small concrete fortifications for machine guns or anti-tank guns). There were also "swimming" tanks, known as D.D.s, that could move through water and climb up onto land to attack fortifications with cannon fire.

Thirty-one D.D. tanks led the British 3d Division onto Sword Beach, the easternmost landing place. Six were knocked out by cannon fire, but within twenty minutes, most of the German defenders had fled or been wiped out, and Sword Beach was in Allied hands.

D.D. tanks were also with the Canadian 3d Division on Juno Beach, but the foot soldiers reached the beach before the tanks did. It was thick with pillboxes, trenches, and fortifications, and filled with German troops, machine guns, and cannons. The Canadians began taking heavy casualties. As D.D.s came onto the beach, groups of men gathered behind them for protection, and moved forward with them. The tanks blew open pillboxes and gun emplacements, and the infantrymen dealt with the enemy soldiers in trenches By noon, the whole Canadian division was ashore and moving forward. But it had lost nearly 1,200 men during the first hour of the landing.

Gold Beach, too, was thick with fortifications, but the gunfire of British warships knocked out many of them. Most of the German troops quickly surrendered, and there were no troops behind them to make a counterattack. The British landing on Gold Beach cost only 400 men.

At Utah Beach, the strong current carried the landing craft more than a mile south of where the American 4th Division troops were supposed to land. But this turned out to be lucky—it brought the division to where there were the fewest German soldiers and fortifications anywhere along the beach. The division's three regiments moved forward and found only a single German regiment in their way. Most of its men surrendered.

More men and vehicles were pouring onto the beach. By nightfall, 23,000 Americans had come onto Utah Beach, and the 4th Division had penetrated 4 miles (6 kilometers) into France.

Midway between Utah and Omaha beaches is an area called Pointe du Hoc. There, the land ends in 100-foot (31-meter)-high cliffs that loom over a narrow area of beach. Some distance back from the cliff edge was a fortification with five German cannons that were a serious threat to the troops that would land on Omaha Beach—the guns would be able to saturate the beach with shellfire. It was to be the job of three companies of the U.S. 2d Ranger Battalion to land at Pointe du Hoc, climb up the cliffs above, with German soldiers shooting down at them, eliminate any enemy troops in their path, and put the German guns out of action.

The top of the cliff was pounded with shellfire from the battleship *Texas* before the rangers landed. But Germans who had hidden in underground shelters rushed to the edge of the cliff and opened fire as the ranger assault boats reached the beach, causing casualties. Two destroyers came in close and opened fire, driving them back.

Grapnels were used to get up the cliff. These were shafts of steel with three curved hooks on the end attached to lengths of rope coiled inside tubes. They were fired by springs that made a twanging noise, and shot out of the tubes up into the air toward the edge of the cliff. Many fell back down, but a few caught fast in clumps of rock and in the barbed wire the Germans had spread along the cliff's edge. Seizing the ropes, rangers climbed hand over hand to the top of the cliff.

Reaching the top, they rushed the fortification, wiping out or capturing the enemy soldiers left. But the guns weren't there! They had been moved.

The rangers went looking for them and located them 1 mile (1.6 kilometers) away and unguarded. They were still a danger, because they could shoot 7 miles (11 kilometers), so the

*American soldiers, packed tightly in an LCP, cross
the English Channel on the morning of D-Day.*

Bicycles in tow, troops of the Canadian 3d Division disembark at Juno Beach, Normandy, France, on D-Day.

rangers put them all out of commission. Then the rangers pulled back to the fortification.

Soon they were attacked. They hung on through the night and the next day, until the attacks ended. Of the 200 rangers who had landed, only fifty were left.

The landing at Utah Beach was fairly easy. The landing at Pointe du Hoc was bloody and desperate, but successful. But Omaha Beach nearly became another Gallipoli.

It was a lot better defended than the Allies had thought. The water in front of it was filled with mines, and so was the sandy beach. A hill sloped up from the beach, and on the hill were pillboxes, steel-and-concrete fortifications, and trenches. Every foot of the land in front of the hill, and hundreds of yards of the water, could be saturated with machine-gun and cannon fire.

Things went wrong from the start. Bombers were supposed to plaster the fortified area before the troops landed, but heavy clouds prevented them from seeing clearly, and they simply missed the target. Ships were supposed to bombard the beach with rockets, but most of the rockets fell short, exploding in the water. Many of the landing craft did not get in close enough and soldiers rushing down the ramps expecting to step onto a sandy beach found themselves having to swim toward a still distant shore. Men with heavy equipment, such as radios, strapped to their bodies plunged straight down into water over their heads and quickly drowned.

The water was boiling with spouts from shell explosions and the impact of bullets, and was quickly becoming dotted with floating bodies. The beach, too, flared with shell explosions and buzzed with machine-gun bullets. Men struggled out of the water, stepped onto the sand, and instantly went down, killed or badly hurt. Survivors hugged the ground or sheltered behind the steel girders the Germans had placed along the shoreline as tank obstacles. Some men managed to reach the long, low sea-wall of pebbles that lay across the beach, and crouched behind it. But there was no forward movement.

So the Allied forces invading Normandy from the sea had gained a toehold on four of the five beaches, where they were slowly moving forward. But on the fifth beach, Omaha, the

U.S. troops hit the beaches of Normandy, June 6, 1944.

American 1st and 29th divisions were pinned down, taking terrible casualties from strong German defenses. If they could not begin to move forward and capture or destroy the enemy fortifications and strongholds, they would be wiped out, and the beach would stay in German hands. This could turn the entire Normandy invasion into a terrible disaster!

But gradually, groups of men managed to crawl over the seawall in places, and sneak forward without getting hit. They wiped out German machine-gun and mortar emplacements with hand grenades. They caught Germans in trenches by surprise, and wiped them out with rifle fire. Slowly, the German fire diminished, and more men were able to move forward, taking out more machine guns and mortars, and beginning to capture fortifications.

Finally, at Omaha Beach progress was being made, and the landing had turned into a success. But 2,200 American soldiers had been killed or wounded.

The successful amphibious invasions at Normandy were the beginning of the end for Germany. Allied troops poured into France and began steadily pushing the German forces back. Nearly a year of fighting remained, but in May of 1945 Germany surrendered, and World War II came to an end in Europe.

Chapter 5

THE LANDING AT INCHON

During World War II, the nation of Korea was occupied and ruled by Japanese troops. With the end of the war, in 1945, all Japanese personnel left Korea, and the country was suddenly on its own, with no government, no law system, no police force, and no money! The United States and the Soviet Union agreed to help Korea get control of itself. The Soviet government took charge of the northern half of the country, the American government took charge of the southern half. They began helping the Koreans form a government, create industries, and establish money systems.

However, the Soviet and American systems of government were totally different. In the American system, democracy, the people cast votes to elect representatives to make the kinds of laws and do the kinds of things most people want. In the Soviet system, communism, the government made all decisions, and

An aerial view of the port of Inchon, Korea, with ships unloading troops and supplies

the people simply had to accept them. The Soviets taught the North Koreans to form a communist government, while the Americans helped the South Koreans become a democracy.

Thus, when the Soviets and Americans left, by 1950, there were actually two separate countries—the People's Republic of Korea in the north, and the Republic of Korea in the south. The names were similar, but they were two completely different forms of government and ways of life, facing each other across a border. And there was dislike and distrust on each side.

On the morning of June 25, 1950, determined to conquer the south and unite all of Korea under communist rule, soldiers of the North Korean army smashed across the border and invaded South Korea. They had been well trained and well equipped by the Soviets, and within a day they destroyed much of the South Korean army, and were on the verge of capturing the South Korean capital city, Seoul.

At the urging of the United States, the United Nations (U.N.), which had been formed after World War II, ordered North Korea to remove its army from the south. North Korea ignored the demand. The U.N. immediately requested that all its members go to South Korea's aid in some way.

The U.N. member with a military force closest to Korea was the United States, which had troops in Japan. U.S. President Harry Truman authorized the American army, navy, and air force to provide help to South Korea. On July 1, the first troops of the U.S. 24th Division were landing in the port of Pusan, at South Korea's southern tip.

Pusan was important. Not only was it a port where troops, tanks, vehicles, and equipment could be landed from ships, but it also had an airfield from which military airplanes could go into action. Thus, it could be a strong base for U.N. forces in Korea to operate against the North Korean army. The 24th Division's job was to defend it from any attempt the North Korean forces might make to capture it.

But the North Korean generals also understood the importance of Pusan, and the North Korean army was heading straight down the peninsula toward it. The 24th Division troops in their path were not strong enough to stop them. By July 19, the 24th Division was in retreat with heavy losses, the North Koreans on their heels.

However, the 24th had held on just long enough to enable more American and some British troops to land in Pusan with tanks and artillery, and U.S. Air Force fighter planes were now on the Pusan airfield. These U.N. forces quickly formed a ring of defense around the port, and met the fierce attack the North Koreans now hurled at them.

On July 8, General Douglas MacArthur, one of America's most respected and successful commanders in World War II, had been appointed supreme commander of U.N. forces in Korea. MacArthur had to do something to take pressure off the U.N. forces at Pusan before they were defeated and the base was lost. He came up with a plan to make a sudden surprise landing of U.N. troops far up the coast *behind* the North Korean army at Pusan. The North Koreans would find themselves suddenly trapped between two forces, with their supplies cut off. The best place to make the landing, MacArthur believed, was a port city called Inchon, on South Korea's west coast, about 150 miles (240 kilometers) from Pusan.

However, Inchon was one of the worst places in the world to make an amphibious landing! Ships bringing the landing force would have to come up a narrow, winding channel leading from the sea to the city, and the North Koreans could fill this with floating mines. A tiny island called Wolmi-do, sitting in the channel less than a mile from Inchon and connected to the city by a causeway, had been fortified and was bristling with guns that could sink ships trying to get past. Wolmi-do would have to be attacked and captured before a landing could be made at Inchon, which would destroy any chance for the Inchon

General Douglas MacArthur

landing to be a surprise. Inchon was in a region occupied by North Korean troops, which could be rushed into the city in large numbers if U.N. troops tried to make a landing.

And the worst obstacle of all would be the tides at Inchon, which rise and fall as much as 32 feet (10 meters) in six hours. Any landing craft still in the water when the tide dropped would be caught in a 2-mile (3-kilometer) stretch of gluey mud, helpless targets for twelve hours. Thus, any invading force would have only two hours to make its landings, seize control of the beach, and bring in enough supplies and ammunition to keep it going for half a day. Many American generals and admirals believed a landing attempt at Inchon would be impossible, and tried to talk MacArthur out of it.

But MacArthur got his way. He received approval from President Truman for the landing, and put together a force of American and British warships and American, British, and South Korean troops, labeled the Tenth Corps. On the morning of September 10, 1950, these U.N. forces struck.

U.S. Marine planes suddenly came roaring over Wolmi-do. They rained down napalm bombs, setting buildings, bushes, brush, and trees on fire. The next day, navy aircraft carrier planes dropped explosive bombs everywhere. Two days later, warships began to pound the island with gunfire, smashing any artillery that tried to fire back. Floating mines bobbing in the channel water were detonated and destroyed by machine-gun fire from the ships.

As some American commanders had feared, this attack alerted the North Korean commander in Inchon to the possibility of a landing. He sent a message to his superiors in Seoul. Luckily for the U.N. force, the message was apparently ignored.

The way to Inchon was now open, but Wolmi-do had to be completely eliminated as a threat. On the morning of September 15, a U.S. Marine battalion stormed onto the island and cleared out all remaining North Korean forces there. The

Waves of marines land upon the shores of Inchon,
then use ladders to scale the seawall.

tide went down, and the ships sat back several miles from the harbor and pounded Inchon with gunfire. The city was soon ablaze with many fires, and a shroud of smoke hung over it.

By 3:30 in the afternoon the tide was up again, and the amphibious invasion of Inchon began, with the landing of two regiments of U.S. Marines and a South Korean marine regiment. They landed on each side of the city, at places labeled Red Beach and Blue Beach, 4 miles (6 kilometers) apart. At Red Beach, a 15-foot (5-meter)-high, 1,000-foot (305-meter)-long stone seawall blocked the way into the city. Equipped with ladders and explosives, the marines climbed over the wall in some places, blew their way through it in others. At Blue Beach, the 14-foot (5-meter)-high wall was handled the same way. Beyond these walls, in trenches and behind barricades, were the North Korean troops defending Inchon. They opened fire, but as the U.N. forces charged them, many simply turned and ran, most others raised their hands in surrender. By dawn of September 16, Inchon was in U.N. hands; 1,350 North Koreans were killed, wounded, or captured, and the marines lost 20 dead and 174 wounded.

The amphibious landing at Inchon was a complete success. What it accomplished was an even greater success. The U.N. forces launched an attack from Inchon and drove North Korean troops out of Seoul. With a U.N. army now between them and their sources of supplies, the North Korean forces at Pusan began to come apart. Some troops surrendered, most began desperately trying to make their way back north. By September 29, the only North Korean soldiers left in South Korea were those who had been taken prisoner. The Inchon landing is regarded as one of the great military operations of history, one that turned a possible defeat into a stunning victory.

There had been invasions from the sea in the centuries before the twentieth century, but it was only in the twentieth century that such invasions were so carefully planned and organized, and so many kinds of craft were invented and built especially for them. They were a major part of the biggest war in history, World War II. It might well be said that the twentieth century was the age of amphibious invasions.

Index

Page numbers in *italics* refer
to illustrations.

Alexander, Harold, *28*
Algeria, 30, 31, 34
ANZACs, 13
Australia, 10, 13

Battleships, 8, *9*
Belgium, 19
Black Sea, 6
Bosporus Strait, 6, *7*, 8

Canada, 49
Casablanca, 32–34
China, 5
Clark, Mark, 44, 45
Communism, 57–58

Dardanelles, 6, 8, 10
D.D. tanks, 49
D-Day, 46–47, *48*, 49–50, *51*, *52*,
    52–53, *54*, 55
Democracy, 57–58
DUKWs, 37–38, *38*, 41

Egypt, 5
Eisenhower, Dwight D., *28*, 29, 47
English Channel, 19, 46
Eniwetak, 27

Fascism, 43
Fiji Islands, 23
First World War, 6–15
Florida Island, 22, 24, 26
France, 8, 10, 12, 17–19, 31–34,
    44, 46, 47

Gaba Tepe, 13
Gallipoli, *4*, 8, *9*, 10, *11*, 12–15,
    14, 20, 23, 45, 53
Gavutu, 22, 26
Germany, 17–19, 29, 31, 34, 35,
    37, 39, 41, 43–47, 49, 50, 52,
    53, 55

Gold Beach, 47, 49
Great Britain, 8, 10, 12–14, 17–20,
    29–34, 37, 39, 44–47, 49, 61
Greece, 5, 35, 37
Guadalcanal, 22–25, *25*, 27
Guam, 27

Higgins boats, 22, 24, 31, 32
Hitler, Adolf, *42*, 43, 46

Inchon, Korea, *56*, 59, 61–63, *62*
Italy, 19, 29, 34, 35, 37, 39, 41, 43–45
Iwo Jima, 27

Japan, 5, 20, 23–27
Juno Beach, 47, 49, *52*

Korean War, 58–59, 61–63, *62*
Kwajalein, 27

LCP (Landing Craft, Personnel),
    20, 40
LCP(R) (Landing Craft,
    Personnel (Ramp)), 20
LCV (Landing Craft, Vehicle), 20,
    22
Leyte, 27
LST (Landing Ship, Tank), *30*,
    38, *39*, *40*
Luzon, 27

MacArthur, Douglas, 59, *60*
Marathon, 5
Mediterranean Sea, 34, 35
Midway Island, battle at, 20, *21*
Montgomery, Sir Bernard, 37, 44
Morocco, 30–34
Mussolini, Benito, *42*, 43

Narrows, 6, 8, 14
Narvik Bay, *16*
Netherlands, 19
New Zealand, 10, 13
Normandy invasion, 46–47, *48*,
    49–50, *51*, *52*, 52–53, *54*, 55

North Africa, 29–34
Norway, 17–18

Okinawa, 27
Omaha Beach, 47, 50, 53, 55
Operation Torch, *28*, 29–34

Pas de Calais, 46
Patton, George, *29*, 34, 37
Pearl Harbor, 20
Peleliu, 27
Philippines, 27
Pointe du Hoc, 50, 52, 53
Poland, 17
Pusan, Korea, 58–59, 63

River Clyde (ship), 10, *11*,
    12
Russia, 6, 8

Saipan, 27
Salerno, 44–45
Sardinia, 35, 37
Sea of Marmara, 6, 8
Sea People, 5
Second World War, 17–55
Sicily, 35, 37–41, 43
Solomon Islands, 22–23
Spain, 35
Sword Beach, 47, 49

Tanambogo, 22, 26
Tarawa, 27
Tiger tanks, 45
Tinian, 27
Trenches, 10, 13
Truman, Harry, 58, 61
Tulagi, 22–24, 26–27
Turkey, 6, 8, 10, 12–15

United States, 20, 22–27, 29–
    33, 37, 39–41, 44–47, *48*,
    49–50, *51*, *53*, 55, 57–59,
    61–63
Utah Beach, 47, 49–50, 53

UNION OF SOVIET SOCIALIST REPUBLICS

INCHON

Red Beach

Inchon

Wolmi-do

Blue Beach

CHINA

Seoul

KOREA

Pusan

Bering

Sea of Okhotsk

Sea of Japan

JAPAN

Tokyo

PACIFIC

Okinawa

Iwo Jima

Midway Island

Taiwan

East China Sea

Philippine Sea

Mariana Islands

Wake

BURMA

SIAM

INDOCHINA

Luzon

PHILIPPINES

Leyte

Tinian — Saipan

Guam

Enewetak

Caroline Islands

Kwajalein

Marshall Islands

MALAYA

Peleliu

Borneo

New Guinea

Tarawa

Gilbert Islands

DUTCH EAST INDIES

SOLOMON ISLANDS

Solomon Islands

Coral Sea

Florida Island

Tulagi

Gavutu & Tanamboro

Guadalcanal

AUSTRALIA